Welcome Dear Guest

Feel Free to Write Down Anything in Your Mind

Enjoy Your Time

Guests

Name

Thoughts

Guests

Name | Thoughts

Did you know that diarrhea is hereditary?

It runs in your genes.

Guests

Name

Thoughts

Guests

Name *Thoughts*

What's the best snack for watching a movie that stinks?

Poopcorn!

Guests

Name

Thoughts

Guests

Name | Thoughts

What do you get if you poop in your overalls?

*Dung-arees***!**

Guests

Name

Thoughts

Guests

Name

Thoughts

"Waiter, what's this fly doing in my soup?

"I think it's pooping, sir!"

Guests

Name

Thoughts

Guests

Name | **Thoughts**

Did you hear about the man who ate 24 cans of alphabet soup?

He has trouble with his vowels

Guests

Name

Thoughts

Guests

Name

Thoughts

I ate four cans of alphabet soup yesterday.

Then I had probably the biggest vowel movement ever.

Guests

Name | Thoughts

Guests

Name | Thoughts

Have you seen the movie Diarrhea?
It leaked so they had to release it early.

Guests

Name

Thoughts

Guests

Name

Thoughts

How do you get the bathroom unlocked in a hurry?

With a doo-key.

Guests

Name

Thoughts

Guests

Name

Thoughts

You never really appreciate what you've got until it's gone.

Toilet paper is a good example.

Guests

Name

Thoughts

Guests

Name | Thoughts

Did you hear about the constipated mathematician?

He worked it out with a pencil.

Guests

Name

Thoughts

Guests

Name

Thoughts

What did one fly say to the other?

Is this stool taken?

Name

Guests

Thoughts

Guests

Name

Thoughts

What's big and brown and behind the wall?

Humpty's Dump.

Guests

Name

Thoughts

Guests

Name

Thoughts

Do you want to hear a poop joke?

Never mind it's too corny.

Guests

Name

Thoughts

Guests

Name | Thoughts

"Waiter, what's this fly doing in my soup?"

"Pooping."

Guests

Name

Thoughts

Guests

Name | Thoughts

What do you call a vegetarian with diarrhea?

Salad Shooter.

Guests

Name

Thoughts

Guests

Name | **Thoughts**

What's brown and firm?

The Brown Family Law Firm

Guests

Name

Thoughts

Guests

Name

Thoughts

What do you call a magical poop?

Poodini.

Guests

Name

Thoughts

Guests

Name | Thoughts

What did the poo say to the fart?

You blow me away.

Guests

Name

Thoughts

Guests

Name | Thoughts

What's brown and rhymes with Snoop?

Dr. Dre.

Guests

Name

Thoughts

Guests

Name

Thoughts

Poop jokes aren't my favorite jokes.

But they're a solid #2

Guests

Name	Thoughts

Guests

Name

Thoughts

I ate four cans of alphabet soup yesterday.

Then I had probably the biggest vowel movement ever.

Guests

Name

Thoughts

Guests

Name

Thoughts

People who tell you that they're constipated

are full of crap.

Guests

Name

Thoughts

Guests

Name

Thoughts

Laughter is the best medicine.

Unless you have diarrhea...

Guests

Name

Thoughts

Guests

Name | Thoughts

Did you hear about the constipated composer?

He had problems with his last movement.

Guests

Name

Thoughts

Guests

Name

Thoughts

Do clown farts smell

funny?

Guests

Name | Thoughts

Guests

Name | Thoughts

Did you hear about the constipated accountant?

He couldn't budget.

Guests

Name

Thoughts

Guests

Name	Thoughts

People say love is the best feeling ever.
But I think finding a toilet when you're having diarrhea is better.

Guests

Name

Thoughts

Guests

Name

Thoughts

Poop is a

crap palindrome.

Guests

Name

Thoughts

Guests

Name | **Thoughts**

If a king farts,

is it a noble gas?

Guests

Name

Thoughts

Guests

Name

Thoughts

Poop Pick Up Line:

My love for you is like diarrhea. I can't hold it in.

Guests

Name

Thoughts

Guests

Name | **Thoughts**

What's brown and sounds like a bell?

Dung.

Guests

Name

Thoughts

Guests

Name | Thoughts

What do you get when you poop in your overalls?

Dung-arees.

Guests

Name	Thoughts

Guests

Name

Thoughts

Children are like farts.

Your own are just about bearable, but everyone else's are horrendous.

Guests

Name

Thoughts

Guests

Name | Thoughts

What did one fly say to the other?

Is this stool taken?

Guests

Name

Thoughts

Guests

Name

Thoughts

What's the true definition of bravery?

Chancing a fart when you know you have diarrhea.

Guests

Name

Thoughts

Guests

Name

Thoughts

When bears poop in the woods,

is the smell un-bear-able?

Guests

Name

Thoughts

Guests

Name

Thoughts

What's big and brown and behind the wall?

Humpty's Dump.

Guests

Name	Thoughts

Guests

Name

Thoughts

I was going to tell you a poop joke

but it's really crappy.

Guests

Name

Thoughts

Guests

Name

Thoughts

What do you call Clark Kent with diarrhea?

Poop-erman.

Guests

Name

Thoughts

Guests

Name

Thoughts

Chuck Norris doesn't flush the toilet.

He scares the shit out of it.

Guests

Name | **Thoughts**

Name

Guests

Thoughts

How do you punish Helen Keller.

You leave the plunger in the toilet.

Guests

Name **Thoughts**

Guests

Name | Thoughts

What happened to the fly on the toilet seat?

It got pissed off

Guests

Name

Thoughts

Guests

Name

Thoughts

Why do ducks have feathers?

To cover there butt quack

Guests

Name | Thoughts

Guests

Name | Thoughts

What did the bottle of conditioner do on the toilet?

Shampoo **!**

Guests

Name	Thoughts

Guests

Name

Thoughts

Why did the toilet roll roll down the hill?

To get to the bottom!

Guests

Name	Thoughts

Guests

Name | Thoughts

Confucius said

a man who stand on toilet is high on pot.

Guests

Name

Thoughts

Guests

Name | Thoughts

What did one piece of toilet paper say to the other?

"I feel really wiped."

Guests

Name

Thoughts

Guests

Name

Thoughts

Do you know the difference between toilet paper and a shower curtan...

So you're the one

Guests

Name

Thoughts

Guests

Name

Thoughts

What did Spock encounter in the Enterprise toilet?

– *The Captain's Log*.

Guests

Name

Thoughts

Guests

Name | Thoughts

Why don't girls poop?

They can't keep their mouths shut long enough to build pressure!

Guests

Name

Thoughts

Guests

Name | Thoughts

If pooping is a call of nature.

Then is farting a missed call?

Made in the USA
Coppell, TX
15 November 2020